GLUTEN
RECIPES

Easy and Delicious Homemade Gluten Free Bread Recipes

Bread.

It's Delicious.

Unfortunately there are people that suffer from celiac disease and other gluten intolerant diseases that cannot enjoy bread. Or at least not until they try some of the delicious gluten free bread recipes in this book!

I wrote this book to share some of the most delicious gluten free bread recipes I have made and tried over the years. I personally do not suffer from celiac disease, but my sister has a gluten sensitivity so I made it my mission to create some delicious bread recipes for her.

I hope it inspires you to try some of these recipes and even put your own spin on them!

I think it is important to give a background on celiac disease as well as side effects of consuming gluten regardless if you have celiac disease or not. I am not a doctor, nor am I giving advice on what you should do, if you suffer from any symptoms or have any questions, contact a medical professional.

Copyright Fresh Publications 2014

Disclaimer

All rights Reserved. No part of this publication or the information in it may be quoted from or reproduced in any form by means such as printing, scanning, photocopying or otherwise without prior written permission of the copyright holder.
Terms of Use: Effort has been made to ensure that the information in this book is accurate and complete, however, the author and the publisher do not warrant the accuracy of the information, text and graphics contained within the book due to the rapidly changing nature of science, research, known and unknown facts and internet. The Author and the publisher do not hold any responsibility for errors, omissions or contrary interpretation of the subject matter herein. This book is presented solely for motivational and informational purposes only.

Table of Contents

What is Celiac Disease?
Gluten Intolerance
Going Gluten Free
Gluten Free Bread
Homemade Gluten Free Flour Blend
Multi Grain Gluten Free Flour Blend
Breakfast Breads
- Bagels
- Banana Bread
- Banana Pancakes
- Croissants
- English Muffins
- Scones
- Sweet Cinnamon Rolls
- Waffles
- Your Favorite Berry Muffins

Lunch and Dinner Bread and Roll Recipes
- Beer Bread
- Biscuits
- Burger Buns
- Challah Bread
- Cornbread
- Dinner Rolls
- Flat Bread
- Flaxseed Bread
- Focaccia Bread
- French Bread
- Garlic Basil Bread
- Green Tomato Bread
- Honey Oat Bread
- Irish Soda Bread
- Italian Artisan Bread
- Multi Grain Bread

- No Rye Rye Bread
- Olive Bread With Rosemary
- Olive Oil Bread
- Pita Bread
- Pizza Dough
- Potato Rolls
- Sesame Bread
- Tortillas
- White Bread

Dessert Breads
- Cinnamon Raisin Bread
- Coffee Cake
- Lemon Poppy Seed Bread
- Pumpkin Bread
- Yellow Cake

Conclusion

What is Celiac Disease?

Celiac disease affects 1 in every 133 Americans. It is an autoimmune disease that damages the small intestine and hampers a person's ability to absorb nutrients. People that are affected with this disease cannot consume gluten without having serious health issues. Because of this, they must go on a gluten free diet.

Gluten is a protein that is found in grains. Examples of grains are wheat, barley, and rye to name a few. If a person with celiac disease consumes gluten, their immune system will react by causing harm to the small intestine and not allow the proper absorption of the nutrients. This can lead to much more serious implications such as osteoporosis, anemia, and other deficiency related diseases.

The cause of celiac disease cannot be pinpointed. However, it is believe that if someone in your family has the disease there is about a 15% change that you will have it. There are certain circumstances that seem to cause the disease, such as pregnancy, stress, or through a viral infection. It is hard to diagnose because most of the symptoms are pretty common. Constipation, gas, weight loss, and diarrhea are only a few examples of the broad range of symptoms.

Gluten Intolerance

Some people do not have celiac disease, but still suffer from some symptoms after the consumption of gluten. Studies are still being done as to why this is, but currently is it known as a gluten intolerance. When these people are able to take gluten out of their diet, they report back feeling much better and not suffering from symptoms any longer.

If you do suffer from any symptoms or have any questions it is recommended to call a doctor immediately.

Going Gluten Free

Taking on a gluten free diet is not an easy task. There are going to be many restrictions, especially if this is new to you. Thankfully, over the past few years, there has been an uptick in gluten free products, such as pastas and breads, so it won't be too dreary. On the following pages I wanted to give some examples of foods that should and should not be consumed if you are going to be following a gluten free diet. This is not a complete list, rather just a starter to give you some ideas.

Foods that ARE Allowed

The following is a list of natural foods that have no been processed in any way. An example of something processed vs. unprocessed would be a chicken breast breaded (gluten) vs. a chicken breast grilled with no marinade or sauce (gluten free):

Beans
Seeds
Nuts
Eggs
Meats
Fish
Poultry
Fruits
Vegetables
Most dairy products

Grains and Starches that ARE Allowed

Again, make sure these are in their natural form, not processed or mixed with other grains or preservatives:

Amaranth
Arrowroot
Buckwheat
Cornmeal
Flaxseed
Rice Flour
Soy Flour
Potato Flour
Hominy
Millet
Quinoa
Rice
Sorghum
Soy
Tapioca

Foods and Grains NEVER allowed

Never consume food or drinks that contain the following:

Barley
Malt
Rye
Triticale
Wheat
Bulgur
Durum Flour
Farina
Graham Flour
Kamut
Semolina
Spelt

Foods that MUST BE LABELED GLUTEN-FREE

The following foods cannot be consumed unless it is specifically written on the containers that they are "Gluten-Free":

Beer
Bread
Candy
Cereal
Cookies
Croutons
Gravy
Pasta
Lunch Meats
Oats
Salad Dressing
Sauces
Soups
Vegetables in a sauce

When shopping, cooking, or doing research on foods, make sure that you take into account cross contamination. Cross contamination happens in manufacturer's facilities, where different foods are processed on the same machines. Most labels will have some kind of warning of cross contamination, but it is up to you to do your own due diligence. There are many examples of where cross contamination can happen in your home. A shared plate, microwave, toaster oven, can all be places where cross contamination can take place.

Important Note on Nutrition

Once you begin a gluten free diet, you may suffer from a lack of vitamin nutrients such as iron, calcium, fiber, and niacin. Grains are loaded with vitamins, so when you stop eating them you will also stop receiving the vitamins from them. Again, the important thing here is to contact a medical professional and have your levels tested.

Gluten Free Bread

On to the delicious part of the book! The following pages include some of the most delicious gluten free bread recipes I have tasted. You will notice that I break the recipes into three subsections, breakfast breads, lunch and dinner breads, and dessert breads. I did this just to offer some organization, but I will say that I have had some dessert breads for breakfast and vice versa.

Before we dig into the recipes I wanted to highlight some of the ingredients you will be using now instead of a gluten containing flour such as wheat. They may not be familiar sounding now, but they will be. Here is a short list of ingredients you will be using throughout this book:

- White rice flour
- Oat flour
- Coconut flour
- Tapioca starch
- Xanthan gum
- Brown rice flour
- Teff flour
- Sorghum flour
- Chickpea flour

Throughout the book, you will find recipes that call for the "Homemade Gluten Free Flour Blend" as well as the "Multi-Grain Gluten Free Flour Blend." I thought it would be easiest to list the recipe for these blends here, so that you can prepare these blends ahead of time.

Note that not all of the recipes call for these specific blends. Some of the bread recipes have different variations on some of the same ingredients as well as different ingredients.

Here are the two main flour blend recipes you will find:

Homemade Gluten Free Flour Blend

Ingredients:

1 cup white rice flour
1 cup oat flour
1 cup coconut flour
1 cup tapioca starch
¼ cup cornstarch
3 tsp xanthan gum

Directions:

1. Place in a plastic container, cover tightly with lid, and shake vigorously until everything is well incorporated.

2. 1 cup of our gluten free flour equals 1 cup of regular flour.

Multi Grain Gluten Free Flour Blend

Ingredients:

2 cups cornstarch
2 cups potato starch
1 ¾ cup brown rice flour
1 ½ cup garbanzo bean flour
1 cup sorghum flour
1 cup tapioca flour
¼ cup teff flour

Directions:

1. Place in a plastic container, cover tightly with lid, and shake vigorously until everything is well incorporated.

2. 1 cup of our gluten free flour equals 1 cup of regular flour.

As I mentioned above, some of the bread recipes will call for a portion of these blends in the recipes, while others will have a list of ingredients to mix together. On to the recipes!

Breakfast Breads

Bagels

Ingredients:

2 active quick dry yeast packets
2 cups water, warm
5 ½ cup gluten free all purpose flour
3 tbsp sugar
2 tsp salt
2 qts boiling water
2 tsp canola oil

Directions:

1. Combine yeast and warm water in a small bowl and let sit for 5-10 minutes.

2. In an electric mixing bowl, combine the dry ingredients: all purpose flour, sugar, and salt and mix until it's formed together well.

3. Slowly pour the yeast mixture into the mixing bowl of dry ingredients and mix on medium speed until dough becomes smooth. Cover bowl and set aside for 10 minutes.

4. After 10 minutes, split the dough into 12 even pieces. Roll each dough piece into the shape of a narrow tube, then wet the ends with warm water and fuse the ends together to form the shape of a bagel. Put each bagel on a

baking sheet and then cover for about 45 minutes or until they have risen about 25%.

5. As dough is rising, pour the 2 qts of water into a large pot along with canola oil and bring to a boil.

6. Preheat oven to 400 F.

7. When you are satisfied with how the bagels have risen, take each one and place in the boiling water/canola oil for about 45 seconds. Place on a pre greased baking sheet.

8. Once all bagels have been poached in water, place the baking sheet in oven for about 15 minutes, or until they start to turn golden.

Banana Bread

Ingredients:

2 cups homemade flour blend
1 tsp baking soda
¼ tsp salt
4 eggs
2 cups banana, super ripe, mashed up
1 cup sugar
½ cup applesauce, unsweetened
1/3 cup canola oil
1 tsp vanilla
½ cup walnuts, chopped

Directions:

1. Preheat oven to 350 F.

2. Lightly grease your 8 inch by 4 inch (or similar size) loaf baking pan.

3. Combine flour blend with baking soda and salt in a mixing bowl.

4. In a separate bowl, whisk the four eggs, with the mashed bananas, sugar, applesauce, canola oil, and vanilla.

5. Combine the dry ingredients with the wet ingredients making sure everything is well incorporated.

6. Spoon into the pre greased loaf pans. Sprinkle the walnuts on top.

7. Place into oven and let bake for about 50 minutes. You will know when they are finished baking when you can stick a toothpick into the center and it comes out clean.

Banana Pancakes

Ingredients:

1 cup oat flour
1 tsp baking powder
1 tsp sea salt
¼ tsp cinnamon
1/8 tsp nutmeg
2 small bananas, ripe
½ cup almond milk
2 tsp maple syrup
1 tbsp coconut oil
1 tsp vanilla

Directions:

1. Grease and preheat large skillet.

2. Combine the oat flour, baking powder, salt, cinnamon, and nutmeg in a mixing bowl.

3. Place bananas, milk, syrup, coconut oil, and vanilla in a food blender and pulse until well incorporated. Pour this mixture into the mixing bowl containing the dry foods.

4. Spoon desired size of pancake into the skillet and cook until it browns on its edges. Flip over and cook until it is cooked through and browned on each side. Do this for the remaining of the batter.

Croissants

Ingredients:

2 cup sorghum flour
½ cup chickpea flour
½ cup almond meal
1 cup tapioca flour
1 cup rice flour
4 tsp xanthan gum
1 ½ tsp salt
4 tsp yeast
¼ cup sugar
1 cup warm water
2 eggs, beaten
8 tbsp butter, melted
12 tbsp butter, chopped into small pieces (pea size)

Directions:

1. In blending bowl, combine the sorghum flour, chickpea flour, almond meal, tapioca flour, rice flour, xanthan gum and salt. Mix until well blended.

2. Remove 1 cup of the above flour mixture and pour into a mixing bowl. Throw the yeast, sugar, milk and eggs into this mixture and blend thoroughly. Then add melted butter and blend until everything is well combined. Set aside.

3. In the original bowl from step 1, add the small pea sized cold butter pieces and mix

together. Then, add the liquid batter from Step 2 and combine until everything is mixed through. Cover and place in the refrigerator for 4 hours.

4. After dough has been in refrigerator for at least 4 hours, remove and set on a rice flour covered surface. Cut dough into 3 equal pieces and roll each of the pieces into a 12 inch circle. Cut each of these circles into 8 wedges.

5. Take one wedge at a time (total 24) and use a rolling pin to flatten each out to about 1/8 inch thick. Once flattened, roll each wedge up to its point and then shape into a slight curve.

6. On a parchment lined baking sheet, lay each croissant and cover with plastic. Let sit for up to 2 hours, or until each has risen and doubled in size.

7. Preheat oven to 400 F.

8. Beat the 2 eggs and then brush each croissant with the egg mixture. Place in the oven and lower temperature to 350 F.

9. Let bake for about 15 minutes, or until they turn golden.

English Muffins

Ingredients:

1 packet of yeast
1 tbsp sugar
½ cup water, warm
2/3 cup tapioca flour
1 1/3 cup white rice flour
½ tsp xanthan gum
2 tsp baking powder
2 tsp baking soda
1 tsp salt
1 ½ cups buttermilk
2 tbsp olive oil
Gluten Free cornmeal

Directions:

1. In small bowl, combine the warmed water (120 F) with yeast and sugar. Let it sit for 10 minutes.

2. In electric mixing bowl combine the dry ingredients: tapioca flour, rice flour, xanthan gum, baking powder, baking soda and salt. Mix everything thoroughly.

3. Place buttermilk in microwave to heat until it is lukewarm. Make sure not to make it too hot, as it will curdle. Pour the lukewarm buttermilk and olive oil into the yeast. Then pour this into the dry ingredient mixing bowl and mix until combined.

4. Cover this bowl and set aside for 8 hours.

5. Preheat a griddle to 300 F (medium-high heat).

6. Preheat oven to 325 F.

7. Take a good size prep plate or dish and pour and spread 1 cup of gluten free cornmeal on it. Then take a good size spoon of the batter and place in in cornmeal, cover completely. Shape the batter into a flattened ball, or shape of an English muffin. Do this with all of the batter.

8. Place on the greased griddle, and let brown on bottom side then flip over and let brown on that side. Should take anywhere from 8-15 minutes per side, depending on your griddle.

9. Once browned on each side, place on a baking sheet and then place in the oven for 25 minutes. Keep a close eye on them to make sure they are cooked through and not burning.

10. Once finished cooking, remove from oven and set aside to cool and slice in half before serving.

Scones

Ingredients:

2 cups homemade flour blend
1/3 cup and 1 tsp sugar
1 tsp baking powder
¼ tsp baking soda
½ tsp salt
8 tbsp butter, grated
1 tsp dried cranberries
1 tsp white chocolate chips
½ cup sour cream
1 egg

Directions:

1. Preheat oven to 400 F.

2. In a mixing bowl, combine dry ingredients of 1/3 cup sugar, baking powder, baking soda, and salt. Make sure these are mixed well before grating on the butter. After you grate all the butter (should be thin shreds) mix everything together with your hands. Then add in the dried cranberries and white chocolate chips.

3. In separate bowl, whisk together the egg and the sour cream.

4. Add the sour cream mixture into the dry ingredients. As you are combining these two together, clumps will form. Keep kneading

together and you will get the dough as you like it.

5. Remove dough from bowl and place on a gluten free floured prep area. Work the dough into an 8 inch circle that should be about ¾ of an inch thick. Pour the remaining 1 tsp of sugar over the top of the dough. Then divide into 8 equal pizza slices.

6. Place each slice onto a paper lined baking sheet and place into oven and let bake for about 15 minutes or until golden.

7. Let cool to a warm temperature and enjoy.

Sweet Cinnamon Rolls

Ingredients:

For Rolls:

1 cup brown rice flour
1 cup sorghum flour
½ cup potato starch
½ cup arrowroot powder
2 tbsp sugar
2 tsp baking powder
½ tsp baking soda
1 ½ tsp xanthan gum
½ tsp salt
1 cup milk
1 tbsp apple cider vinegar
¼ cup coconut oil, warm
2/3 cup pumpkin puree
½ tsp vanilla

For Filling:

1 cup chopped dates
¼ cup maple syrup
1 ½ tsp cinnamon
Pinch of salt

For Icing:

¼ cup coconut butter
2 tbsp milk
¼ tsp vanilla
1 tbsp maple syrup

Directions:

1. Preheat oven to 425 F.

2. Prepare a cake pan by greasing bottom and sides.

3. Lay parchment paper across table for preparation and sprinkle with ½ cup of brown rice flour.

4. Mix together milk and apple cider vinegar in small bowl and set aside for 15 minutes.

For dough:

5. In a large bowl, combine the brown rice flour, sorghum flour, potato starch, arrowroot powder, sugar, baking powder, baking soda, xanthan gum, and salt.

6. In a separate bowl combine the milk vinegar mixture with the warmed coconut oil (not heated through, just warm), pumpkin puree, and vanilla. Whisk everything together until well incorporated.

7. Combine the two bowls, mixing the dry ingredients with the wet ingredients. Make sure to combine everything well as this is the dough.

8. Place dough on the prepared parchment paper and knead it thoroughly, making sure to add in the brown rice flour that was already on

the parchment paper. Once its kneaded well, form it into a ½ inch thick rectangle.

For Filling:

9. Combine all of the filling ingredients into your blender and pulse until they are well incorporated and smooth. Pour this on top of the dough rectangle and spread evenly throughout, leaving about an inch from the sides, like a pizza.

10. Carefully, roll the dough using the parchment paper as a guide by lifting it as you move. There is no rush, take your time and do it carefully.

11. After all the dough is rolled, slice into 2 inch pieces, then place these into the pre greased cake pan.

12. Place in oven for 20 minutes, until browned on the edges. Remove from oven and set aside to cool.

For Icing:

13. As rolls are cooling, melt the coconut butter by placing it in a small bowl in hot water for a few minutes. After it has melted whisk in the milk, vanilla, and syrup until it forms a nice icing.

14. Pour on top of rolls and enjoy!

Waffles

Ingredients:

1 ¼ cup almond milk
1 tsp apple cider vinegar
¼ cup vegan butter, melted
1 ½ tsp vanilla
2 tbsp maple syrup
1 cup brown rice flour
½ cup gluten free rolled oats
½ cup potato starch
¼ cup tapioca flour
1 tbsp flaxseed meal
1 ½ tsp baking powder
2 tbsp sugar
Pinch of salt

Directions:

1. Preheat waffle maker.

2. In a small bowl, combine the almond milk and apple cider vinegar and set aside for a couple of minutes. After a couple of minutes whisk in the melted vegan butter, vanilla and maple syrup. Set aside.

3. In separate bowl, add the brown rice flour, rolled oats, potato starch, tapioca flour, flaxseed meal, baking powder, sugar, and salt and combine thoroughly.

4. Mix in the wet ingredients into the bowl with the dry ingredients and mix together.

5. Spoon desired amount into your preheated oven and pre greased waffle maker and serve when ready.

Your Favorite Berry Muffins

Ingredients:

1 ½ cup homemade flour blend
½ tsp salt
2 tsp baking powder
½ tsp cinnamon
1/8 tsp nutmeg
2 tbsp flax seeds, ground
6 tbsp water
2 tbsp maple syrup
1 tsp vanilla
1 ½ tsp apple cider vinegar
1 cup apple sauce, unsweetened
2 tsp water
1 cup strawberries, diced up (can use any berry you like)

Directions:

1. Preheat oven to 400 F.

2. Line muffin pan.

3. Combine the ground flax seeds with 6 tbsp of water in a bowl and let sit for 5 minutes.

4. Combine your homemade flour blend with the salt, baking powder, cinnamon and nutmeg in a large mixing bowl and ensure everything is well incorporated.

5. Take the bowl of the water and flax seed mixture and add the maple syrup, vanilla

extract, apple sauce, water, and apple cider vinegar. Stir everything thoroughly.

6. Create a hole in the center of the dry ingredients (flour) and pour the wet ingredients into the hole. Mix the dry and wet ingredients well, making sure everything is well combined.

7. Toss in the diced strawberries and continue mixing.

8 Spoon mixture into muffin pan liners about 75% full.

9. Place in oven for about 20 minutes. Muffins are done when you can poke a fork into center of one, and it comes out clean.

10. Enjoy.

Lunch and Dinner Bread and Roll Recipes

Beer Bread

Ingredients:

3 eggs, room temperature
3 tbsp olive oil
1 tsp apple cider vinegar
2 tbsp honey
2 ¾ cup homemade flour blend
¼ cup brown rice flour
1 tsp salt
1 tbsp sugar
10 oz., gluten free ale, try Omission
2 ¼ tsp active yeast
Sesame seeds to sprinkle on top
Coconut milk to brush top of loaf

Directions:

1. Grease a loaf baking pan.

2. In an electric mixing bowl, combine eggs, olive oil, and apple cider vinegar, whisking everything together thoroughly.

3. In separate bowl combine the homemade gluten free flour mix, brown rice flour, salt and sugar.

4. Slowly add the dry ingredients to the electric mixing bowl containing the wet ingredients and

turn mixer on slow. After all dry ingredients are added, slowly pout in the gluten free ale and continue mixing on low until well incorporated. Finally, add yeast and continue mixing on low for another 30 seconds or so until smooth. Then turn mixing speed to high and mix for 4 more minutes. The end result will be a thin somewhat wet dough, this is ok.

5. Pour this dough into the pre-greased loaf pan until it is half full. Then brush the coconut milk over the top and sprinkle with sesame seeds. Lightly cover and leave in a warm area to rise for about 45 minutes.

6. Preheat oven to 375 F.

7. Place loaf pan in oven and let bake for 45 minutes. Check regularly after 30 minutes to make sure it is not overcooking. Final result should have a nice golden color and crust. If you have a food thermometer it should read 205 F.

8. Let it cool before enjoying.

Biscuits

Ingredients:

3 ½ cup homemade flour blend
¼ cup sugar
4 tsp baking powder
1 tsp salt
1 cup butter, cold, diced
4 eggs
2/3 cup almond milk

Directions:

1. In bowl, combine dry ingredients: gluten free flour, sugar, baking powder, and salt.

2. Mix in the diced butter pieces and work together with your hands until they are the size of a pea.

3. In separate bowl whisk eggs and almond milk together, then add to the dry ingredients. Combine thoroughly until a nice dough forms.

4. Remove the dough from the bowl and place on a gluten free floured prep area.

5. Roll the dough until it is about ½ inch thick. Then fold the dough lengthwise into thirds. Then fold it into thirds crosswise. Roll the dough out again to about a ½ inch thickness, and repeat the folding process 3 more times to really work the dough.

6. Next, take a cookie cutter pattern, shaped as a biscuit, and cut biscuits out of the dough and place on a pre-greased baking sheet.

7. Preheat oven to 400 F.

8. Place the biscuits on the baking sheet into the freezer for 20 minutes.

9. After 20 minutes remove from freezer and place into the oven and bake for 20 minutes, until golden.

10. Enjoy warm!

Burger Buns

Ingredients:

2 cups brown rice flour
1 cup tapioca flour
1 tbsp instant yeast
1 tbsp xanthan gum
1 ½ tsp salt
2 tsp sugar
1 cup water, warm
4 eggs
1 ¼ cup olive oil
1 tsp apple cider vinegar
Sesame seeds

Directions:

1. In a large electric mixer mixing bowl combine all of the dry ingredients (brown rice flour through sugar).

2. In a separate bowl whisk together the 4 eggs and warm water. Add olive oil and vinegar once this is thoroughly combined.

3. Create a divide in the dry ingredients and slowly add the wet ingredients to this bowl. Once everything is incorporated mix together on high for 2-3 minutes. Dough should have a nice softness to it, but not be runny. If that is the case, add a little flour at a time.

4. Lightly grease a baking pan.

5. Using a half cup measuring cup, spoon out a portion of dough and place on baking pan. Shape into the size of a hamburger bun. Do this with remaining dough.

6. Set aside and let rise for 40 minutes.

7. Preheat oven to 400 F.

8. Once risen, lightly brush tops with olive oil and then sprinkle sesame seeds.

9. Place in oven and let bake for 12 minutes. Keep a close eye as they will bake fast, and you do not want them to burn. You will know they are done when tops have a nice golden brown look.

10. Remove from oven, let cool, and enjoy with a delicious burger.

Challah Bread

Ingredients:

2 cups rice flour
1 ¾ cups tapioca flour
¼ cup + 2 tsp sugar
3 tsp xanthan gum
½ tsp salt
2/3 cup + 1 cup warm water
1 ½ tbsp yeast
4 tbsp butter, melted
1 tsp apple cider vinegar
4 eggs, beaten

Directions:

1. In an electric mixing bowl combine all of the dry ingredients, rice flour through salt, EXCEPT for 2 tsp of sugar.

2. Take the 2 tsp of sugar and pour that into 2/3 cup of warm water along with the yeast. Set it aside for 5 minutes to foam.

3. In a separate mixing bowl, combine the melted butter with the apple cider vinegar and remaining 1 cup of water.

4. Turn the electric mixer on low speed and mix the dry ingredients. Slowly add in the butter/water, as well as the eggs. After you pour eggs in and they are incorporated add the yeast mixture and turn mixer on high for 2 minutes.

5. Set bowl aside and lightly cover. Let it rise for about an hour.

6. Grease loaf pan.

7. After the hour of rising, place back on mixer and mix on high for 3 more minutes. Spoon dough into the pre-greased loaf pan, and let it rise for another 40 minutes.

8. Preheat oven to 400 F and place loaf pan inside to bake for about 60 minutes, or until golden.

Cornbread

Ingredients:

2 eggs, beaten
1 ½ water, warm
¼ cup vegetable oil
1 ½ cup cornmeal
1 cup millet flour
1 cup rice flour
¼ cup sugar
1 tbsp baking powder
1 tsp salt

Directions:

1. Preheat oven to 400 F.

2. Grease baking pan.

3. Mix together the beaten eggs with warmed water and vegetable oil in a small bowl, set aside.

4. In a large mixing bowl combine the cornmeal, millet flour, rice flour, sugar, baking powder, and salt. Once everything is mixed well, create a divide in the center and add in the egg mixture. Mix until everything is well combined.

5. Move batter to the pre-greased baking pan and place in oven to bake for 20 minutes. Cornbread should have a nice golden color to it.

6. Remove from oven to cool.

Dinner Rolls

Ingredients:

2 ¾ cup homemade flour blend
2 tsp instant yeast
¼ cup sugar
1 tsp salt
1 cup water, warm
2 tbsp butter, melted
1 egg, beaten
1 tsp apple cider vinegar

Directions:

1. In an electric mixer mixing bowl, combine homemade gluten free flour blend, instant yeast, sugar, and salt. Turn mixer on low, and add warmed water, melted butter, egg and the apple cider vinegar. After everything has been added, turn speed to high and mix for 3 minutes.

2. Lightly spray a round cake pan with cooking spray. Then, using a 1/3 cup measuring cup, scoop out a portion of dough and place it right in the center of the cake pan. Then continue by scooping 8 more scoops of dough and lining them up around the center scoop.

3. These rolls are going to be easy to pull apart, but to make divisions wet your fingers with warm water and smooth out the tops of the dough and make sure to have a decent separation between each scoop of dough, they

will rise and connect, but it will be easier to separate into pieces by taking this step.

4. After everything is smooth, cover with a dry towel and let rise for 1 hour.

5. Preheat oven to 400 F.

6. Bake in oven for 25 minutes, or until tops of rolls have a nice golden brown look.

7. Remove from oven, let cool slightly, and enjoy.

Flat Bread

Ingredients:

1 cup rice flour
2 tbsp oil
½ tsp salt
2 cups water
½ cup rice flour (prepping)

Directions:

1. In a pot, bring oil, salt, and water to a bowl. As it begins boiling, adjust heat to low and add the cup of rice flour. Stir until the dough forms. Remove from heat and let cool until you can handle with your hands.

2. Pour dough into a large mixing bowl and knead it with your hands until it starts to hold together well.

3. Place a skillet over low-medium heat, as you will start to prepare your first flat bread.

4. Remove a gold sized bowl of dough and work it into a small flat circle shape, very thin. Take this flat bread and transfer it to the skillet that is now warm over the low-medium heat. Let it sit for about a minute, or until bubbles begin to form. Once this happens, flip it over and repeat for another minute. Flip it once more for about 20 seconds until it begins to brown, and repeat on the other side.

5. Repeat for the remaining dough and enjoy your flatbreads!

Flaxseed Bread

Ingredients:

2 cups flax seed meal
1 tbsp baking powder
1 tsp salt
1 tbsp sugar
5 eggs, beaten
½ cup water
1/3 cup oil

Directions:

1. Preheat oven to 350 F.

2. Place greased parchment paper on a baking sheet.

3. In a large mixing bowl, combine the flax seed meal, baking powder, salt and sugar. Once mixed together well, add the 5 beaten eggs, water, and oil to this mixture and continue to combine thoroughly.

4. Let sit for 2 minutes and then pour onto the prepared baking sheet making sure to spread evenly throughout.

5. Place in oven and let bake for 20 minutes until a nice golden brown color appears.

6. Remove from oven and let cool before slicing into it.

Focaccia Bread

Ingredients:

1 Yukon gold potato, peeled sliced into quarters
2 ¼ tsp active dry yeast
1 tbsp sugar
1 cup water, warm
1 cup tapioca flour
¾ cup sorghum flour
2/3 cup potato starch
½ cup sweet rice flour
1 tsp xanthan gum
½ tsp guar gum
2 tsp sea salt
1 egg, separate yolk from white
3 tbsp olive oil
2 tsp rosemary, minced

Directions:

1. Place the peeled potato quarters into a pot with water and sea salt. Bring to a boil and continue cooking for about 20 minutes, or until you can stick a fork into the potato and it comes out smooth and easily. Remove from heat, drain potato, and set aside to cool for a few minutes. Once it has cooled enough, use a fine mesh sieve on the potato quarters to reduce it to a pulp.

2. In a bowl, combine yeast with sugar and warmed water. Let proof for about 10 minutes.

3. In an electric mixing bowl, add the tapioca flour, sorghum flour, potato starch, sweet rice flour, xanthan gum, guar gum, and salt. Make sure to mix everything together well.

4. Next, you are going to add the wet ingredients to the dry in the mixing bowl: egg yolk, olive oil, yeast water, potato rice (from step 1) and rosemary. Turn the mixer on medium speed and let it work for about 5 minutes. After 5 minutes you should have a nice bowl of dough with a cake batter consistency.

5. You are now going to add the egg white to the dough after you beat it. Make sure everything is well combined and then set the bowl aside for at least an hour to let it rise and double in size.

6. Preheat oven to 450 F.

7. Line a baking sheet with parchment paper and grease the paper.

8. Lay the dough on the parchment paper and flatten it out to your desired thickness. Place baking sheet into the oven on the middle rack. On the bottom rack place an oven safe skillet filled with ice cubes.

9. Let bake for 25-30 minutes, or until the top is golden brown and internal temperature hit 180 F.

10. Remove from oven, place on wire rack, let cool for 30-45 minutes and enjoy.

French Bread

Ingredients:

2 cups white rice flour
1 cup tapioca flour
3 tsp xanthan gum
1 ½ tsp salt
2 tbsp sugar
1 ½ cup water, room temperature
2 tbsp yeast, fast rise
2 tbsp butter, melted
3 egg whites, beaten
1 tsp vinegar

Directions:

1. In bowl pour sugar into water and add yeast. Set aside.

2. Grease cookie sheets or French bread shaped pans.

3. In an electronic mixing bowl, place white rice flour, tapioca flour, xanthan gum, and salt and blend until well incorporated. Once well incorporated pour the yeast mixture into this dry mixture and continue blending.

4. Next, add butter, egg whites, and vinegar and blend for another 4-5 minutes.

5. Preheat oven to 400 F.

6. Spoon this mixture onto the pre greased cookie sheets, in French bread shape, or French bread shaped pans. Make slight cuts every couple of inches on top of the dough. Cover it and place and let sit for 20 minutes to let it rise.

7. Once it has risen, and doubled in size, place in oven for 45 minutes.

8. Remove from oven and let cool.

Garlic Basil Bread

Ingredients:

6 cups homemade flour blend
1 tbsp xanthan gum
1 tsp salt
3 tbsp fresh basil, minced
1 tsp pepper
1 ½ tsp garlic powder
2 tbsp yeast
2 eggs, beaten
4 tbsp butter
2 tbsp honey
2 cup buttermilk, warm
¾ cup water, warm
2 tsp apple cider vinegar

Directions:

1. Preheat oven to 350 F.

2. In an electric mixer mixing bowl, combine all of the dry ingredients: flour through garlic powder. Mix together.

3. In a skillet over medium heat, place buttermilk and water until they are warm, but not hot or boiling. Add the yeast to this and set aside for 5 minutes. Then pour into the dry ingredients along with the eggs, honey, butter and apple cider vinegar. Mix on high for 4 minutes.

4. Lightly grease 2 loaf pans. Spoon the batter into the loaf pans and smooth it out by wetting your fingers to work it.

5. Place in the oven and bake for 18 minutes. Remove from oven after 18 minutes; brush the tops with melted butter and place back in the oven and bake for another 20 minutes.

6. Remove from oven and place on a rack to cool in the loaf pans for 10 minutes. After 10 minutes remove from loaf pan and let cool on their own before enjoying.

Green Tomato Bread

Ingredients:

5 green tomatoes
1/3 cup water
¼ cup raisins
1/3 cup vegetable shortening
1 1/3 cup sugar
2 eggs
1 3/4 cup homemade flour blend
1 tsp baking soda
¾ tsp salt
¼ tsp gluten free baking powder
½ tsp cinnamon
½ tsp cloves
1/3 cup pecans, chopped

Directions:

1. Grease a loaf baking pans.

2. Preheat oven to 350 F.

3. Slice and dice up the green tomatoes and then place them in a food blender and pulse until smooth and creamy. You are going to use 1 cup of this pulp for the recipe.

4. In a pot, bring the 1/3 cup of water to a boil. Once boiling, place raisins in water and let soak for 3 minutes. Remove from heat and set aside.

5. In a large mixing bowl, combine the vegetable shortening, sugar, and eggs. Beat everything together thoroughly and then add the 1 cup of green tomato pulp, and raisins with the water. Continue mixing until everything is combined.

6. In a separate mixing bowl, combine the dry ingredients: gluten free flour, baking soda, salt, baking powder, cinnamon, cloves, and pecans. After everything is mixed together, begin slowly adding ½ cup of this to the mixing bowl containing the wet ingredients, stirring well each time.

7. Spoon dough into the pre-greased loaf baking pan, and use wet fingers to smooth it out.

8. Place in oven and let bake for 60 minutes. After 60 minutes, remove from oven, and let cool before slicing into it.

Honey Oat Bread

Ingredients:

4 cups gluten free oats
2 tbsp yeast
1 ½ cup water, warm
¼ cup olive oil
¼ cup honey
2 tbsp honey
½ cup tapioca flour
½ cup white rice flour
2 tsp xanthan gum
1 tsp salt
¼ tsp cinnamon
4 eggs

Directions:

1. Lightly grease a bread loaf pan.

2. In a blender, place 4 cups of oats and blend until extremely fine.

3. In small bowl, combine the yeast and the warmed water. Set aside for 5 minutes.

4. In large mixing bowl, combine the ground up oats with the yeast water, olive oil, honey, tapioca flour, white rice flour, and xanthan gum and mix until everything is thoroughly incorporated. Then add salt, cinnamon, and eggs and continue mixing until you have a fluffy dough mixture.

5. Pour mixture into the pre-greased loaf pan and let rise for about 40 minutes, until it has doubled in size.

6. Preheat oven to 350 F, about 10 minutes before dough is finished rising.

7. Make a few ¼ inch slits in the top part of dough and then sprinkle oats on top as well.

8. Place in oven for 45 minutes.

9. Let cool before slicing and enjoying.

Irish Soda Bread

Ingredients:

1 ½ cups white rice flour
½ cup tapioca flour
½ cup sugar
1 tsp baking soda
1 tsp baking powder
1 tsp salt
1 egg
1 cup buttermilk

Directions:

1. Preheat oven to 350 F.

2. Lightly grease a round cake pan.

3. In a large mixing bowl combine the dry ingredients (white rice flour through salt) and combine thoroughly.

4. In a separate bowl combine the egg and buttermilk, whisking together.

5. Create a divide in the center of the dry ingredients and pour the wet ingredients inside. Gently fold over and mix together until everything is moistened. Pour this mixture into the pre-greased cake pan.

6. Place in oven and let bake for 1 hour. After an hour, check on bread by inserting a knife into the center and pulling it out. If it comes out

clean, the bread has cooked through, if it is still moist and comes out with residue on it, continue baking for 5 more minutes and then check again.

7. Remove from oven, place on wire rack and let cool for 10 minutes. After 10 minutes, remove the bread from the baking pan and continue to let cool. Let it stand for 6-8 hours before consuming, so flavor can settle.

Italian Artisan Bread

Ingredients:

¾ cup potato starch
¼ cup brown rice flour
¼ cup homemade flour blend
¼ cup tapioca starch
1/8 cup buckwheat flour
1 tbsp sweet rice flour
1 tsp xanthan gum
1 tsp guar gum
½ tsp pectin
¾ tsp salt
1 tsp goat milk, powdered
½ cup water, warm
1 tsp honey
½ tbsp. active dry yeast
1 tsp honey
2 eggs, beaten
1/8 cup canola oil

Directions:

1. Combine all of the dry ingredients (potato starch through powdered goat milk) in an electric mixing bowl set up. Make sure everything is mixed well.

2. In a separate bowl, combine the warm (not hot) water with the yeast and 1 tsp of honey and let sit for 10 minutes.

3. After 10 minutes, add the yeast mixture along with the remaining honey, beaten eggs,

and canola oil to the dry ingredients in the mixing bowl. Mix on medium speed using a dough hook until dough becomes smooth and springy. If it is too dry add warm water 1 tsp at a time.

4. Take the bowl off the mixing stand, cover, and set aside for 30 minutes.

5. Prep a flat cooking surface with gluten free flour. We are going to work the dough on this. After 30 minutes, remove dough from bowl and place on this surface. Roll it around gently so that the entire ball of dough has some of this flour covering it.

6. Prep a baking sheet with a piece of parchment paper that is lightly greased.

7. Once it is covered, begin stretching it out into the shape of an oval. Once you have the desired shape, place it on the prepped baking sheet. Rub the canola gently over the dough and make some shallow cuts on top of the dough.

8. Place in the oven (which we did not preheat on purpose) and turn the temperature to 400 F. Set the timer for 48 minutes and let bake. After 48 minutes the bread should have a nice brown to it.

9. Let cool and enjoy.

Multi Grain Bread

Ingredients:

2 ¼ cups Multi Grain Gluten Free flour
¼ cup amaranth flour
¼ cup teff flour
¼ oz (1 package) active dry yeast
1 tbsp xanthan gum
1 tsp salt
1 ¼ cups milk, warm
¼ cup butter, melted
2 eggs, beaten
2 tbsp honey
1 tsp apple cider vinegar
2 tbsp millet
2 tbsp toasted pumpkin seeds
2 tbsp sunflower seeds
2 tbsp ground flax

Directions:

1. Prepare a loaf baking pan by lightly greasing and lining it with parchment paper.

2. In a bowl, combine the first 6 ingredients (**multi grain flour** through **salt**) making sure to mix them together well.

3. In a separate bowl combine the milk, butter, eggs, honey, and apple cider vinegar and whisk together thoroughly. Once mixed together, slowly add the flour mixture to this mixture, mixing as you combine. Then add the millet, pumpkin seeds, sunflower seeds, and

flax and continue mixing until everything is thoroughly combined.

4. Place dough in the pre greased loaf baking pan and smooth out the top. Lightly cover the dough and set aside for 45 minutes.

5. Preheat oven to 375 F.

6. Place bread in oven for 40 minutes, until is has a nice brown color. After 40 minutes, remove the pan from the oven, remove bread from loaf pan, but keep it on parchment paper and place the paper with bread on top back into oven for another 5 minutes.

7. Remove from oven, and let cool before enjoying.

No Rye Rye Bread

Ingredients:

1 cup sorghum flour
1 cup potato starch
½ cup millet flour
2 tsp xanthan gum
1 ¼ tsp sea salt
2 tbsp cocoa, natural unsweetened
2 tsp orange peel, grated
2 tsp caraway sees
1 tsp dried onion, minced
½ tsp dill
1 packet rapid dry yeast

1 ¼ cup water, warm
1 tsp sugar
4 tbsp olive oil
½ tsp lemon juice
2 tbsp honey
2 eggs, beaten

Directions:

1. Add all of the dry ingredients (sorghum flour through dill) together in a large mixing bowl and combine thoroughly.

2. In a separate bowl combine yeast with warm water and sugar. Set aside and let the yeast foam for about 10 minutes.

3. After 10 minutes, create a divide in the bowl containing the dry ingredients and slowly add the yeast along with the olive oil, lemon juice, honey, and beaten eggs. Thoroughly combine together until a dough forms.

4. In a lightly greased loaf pan, spoon the dough and smooth with your fingers. Sprinkle with sesame seeds and cover for 30 minutes to let dough rise.

5. As dough is finishing rising, preheat oven to 350 F.

6. Place the dough into the oven and let it bake for 40 minutes. Keep a close eye on it, you will know it is finished when you knock on it and hear a hollow thump.

Olive Bread With Rosemary

Ingredients:

1 cup brown rice flour
¾ cup sorghum flour
1 ½ cups tapioca flour
1 tbsp active dry yeast
1 ½ tsp salt
1 tbsp xanthan gum
1 1/3 cups water, warmed
2 eggs
2 tbsp canola oil
2 tsp canola oil
1 tbsp honey
½ cup kalamata olives, sliced
2 sprigs rosemary, minced
Olive oil
Pinch of sea salt

Directions:

1. Combine all dry ingredients: brown rice flour through xanthan gum, in an electric mixer mixing bowl and mix together.

2. Create a divide in the dry ingredients and then add the warmed water (about 110 F), beaten eggs, all canola oil, and honey and fold over into the dry ingredients. Turn mixer on low-medium speed for a few minutes until dough begins to form. Once it starts becoming cohesive, toss in the sliced kalamata olives and the rosemary and continue mixing for another 3 minutes.

3. Once everything is well incorporated, move to a large bowl, cover, and let rise for a couple of hours.

4. After dough has risen, divide it in half. You can place other half in the fridge for up to a week if you decide to only bake half for now. Shape the dough into an oval loaf shape, using wet fingers so it won't stick to your hands. Let it sit for 40 minutes.

5. Preheat oven to 450 F.

6. Place parchment paper on a baking sheet and place dough on the paper. Create a few ¼ inch cuts on top of the dough and then sprinkle olive oil and sea salt on top.

7. Place in the oven and let bake for 30-35 minutes, or until bread is firmed and internal temperature reaches 180 F.

8. Remove from oven and let cool.

Olive Oil Bread

Ingredients:

½ cup brown rice flour
¼ cup soy flour
½ cup tapioca starch
1 ¾ cup cornstarch
1 tbsp active yeast
½ tbsp. salt
1 tbsp xanthan gum
1 ¼ cup water, warm
2 eggs
¼ cup olive oil
¼ cup canola oil
1 tsp apple cider vinegar
Sesame seeds to sprinkle
Flaxseeds to sprinkle

Directions:

1. In a large mixing bowl, combine all of the dry ingredients: brown rice flour through xanthan gum. Mix until everything is combined.

2. Then add the remaining ingredients except for the sesame seeds and flaxseeds. Make sure to incorporate everything thoroughly if you are working by hand. If you have a mixer let it work on medium for 3-4 minutes.

3. On a gluten free floured prep area, divide this dough into 2 equal pieces. Wet your hands, and work each piece until you can get it into the desired oval shape. When you have

your desired shape, loosely cover each dough mound and let sit for about an hour to rise.

4. Preheat oven to 450 F.

5. Sprinkle sesame seeds and flaxseeds on top of each loaf. Then place on a parchment paper lined baking sheet and place in oven to bake for 30 minutes.

6. Bread should have nice golden look once ready. Remove from oven and let cool before enjoying.

Pita Bread

Ingredients:

1 egg
¼ cup water, warm
1 tbsp butter, melted
1 tbsp coconut flour, pack tightly
¼ cup almond flour, pack tightly
1/8 tsp salt
1/8 tsp baking soda

Directions:

1. Preheat oven to 350 F.

2. In bowl, whisk together the egg, with water and melted butter. Once mixed thoroughly add the coconut flour, almond flour, salt and baking soda and mix together until it forms a nice batter.

3. On a parchment paper lined baking sheet, divide the batter into 2 even portions and form until each is about 6 inches in diameter.

4. Place baking sheet in oven and let bake for 20 minutes.

5. Remove and let cool before enjoying.

Pizza Dough

Ingredients:

¾ cup Homemade Gluten Free Flour Blend
¾ cup tapioca flour
2 tbsp buttermilk powder
1 tsp gelatin powder, unflavored
1 tsp salt
2 tsp xanthan gum
1 package active dry yeast
1 tsp sugar
2 tsp olive oil
1 ½ tsp apple cider vinegar
½ cup water, lukewarm
Tapioca flour, on hand for rolling
Gluten free cornmeal, for prepping baking sheet

Directions:

1. Preheat oven to 400 F.

2. Prepare a baking sheet by lining it with parchment paper and sprinkling with gluten free cornmeal.

3. In a large electric mixing bowl combine the flour mix, tapioca flour, buttermilk powder, gelatin powder, salt, xanthan gum, yeast, and sugar. Make sure everything is thoroughly mixed together.

4. Next, add the sugar, apple cider vinegar, and olive oil. Work this together and then

slowly begin adding lukewarm water as you continue mixing together.

5. Turn mixer on high for 3 minutes.

6. Prepare a flat cooking area by placing and spreading tapioca flour out. Place dough onto the cooking area and work tapioca flour into the dough, until you are able to form into a nice ball. Do not be shy with the tapioca flour, it is a crucial ingredient here to make sure we can shape the dough correctly.

7. Take a rolling pin and roll the dough out to your desired thickness. *At this point feel free to cut the dough in half or pieces if you want to make smaller pizzas vs. 1 large pizza.*

8. Place pizza dough onto the prepared baking sheet and place in oven for 5 minutes.

9. Remove from oven, place your ingredients on pizza and throw back in oven for another 10 minutes.

10. Enjoy!

Potato Rolls

Ingredients:

1 cup water, warm
2 packets active dry yeast
2 cup mashed potatoes, warmed
¼ cup sugar
1 ¼ cup milk
¼ cup vinegar
3 tbsp butter, melted
3 tbsp vegetable oil
2 tsp salt
5 ½ cups homemade flour blend

Directions:

1. In a electric mixer mixing bowl, combine the water, active dry yeast, mashed potatoes, and sugar. Let sit for 10 minutes.

2. In a separate bowl combine the milk, vinegar, melted butter, vegetable oil, and salt. Combine thoroughly. Once combined, add this to the mixing bowl with ingredients from step 1 and mix. Then add flour and mix on high for 5 minutes until a smooth dough or batter forms.

3. Prep a work area by sprinkling homemade gluten free flour blend. Place the dough on the surface and roll it out with a rolling pin to ¾ inch thick dough.

4. With a 2 inch cookie cutter, cut out portions of dough and place on a parchment paper lined

baking sheet. Leave some space between each one. Once all dough has been portioned, cover, and let sit for 15 minutes.

5. Preheat oven to 375 F.

6. Once dough has finished rising, place in oven for 15 minutes. Keep an eye on them, you will know they are done when there is a nice golden finish.

Sesame Bread

Ingredients:

3 tbsp butter
4 tbsp sesame seeds
½ tsp gelatin, unflavored and powdered
1 tsp sugar
2 ¼ tsp active dry yeast
3 eggs
¼ cup buttermilk
1 tbsp molasses
½ cup tapioca flour
6 tbsp chickpea flour
¼ cup almond flour
¼ cup coconut flour
¼ cup amaranth flour
¼ cup sorghum flour
2 tbsp yellow cornmeal
2 tbsp potato flour
2 tbsp cornstarch
1 ½ tsp xanthan gum
¾ tsp salt

Directions:

1. Preheat oven to 425 F.

2. Lightly grease loaf pan.

3. Melt butter in skillet over medium heat. Once just melted add the sesame seeds and sauté for 3-4 minutes, until you can enjoy the smell. Remove from heat, place in bowl and set aside to cool.

4. Combine gelatin and 2 tbsp of cold water in a bowl and let sit for 5 minutes.

5. In a separate larger mixing bowl, combine the sugar, ½ cup of warm water, and yeast. Let this sit for 5 minutes before adding 2 of the eggs, buttermilk, molasses, sesame seed butter, and gelatin mixture. Whisk thoroughly until all these ingredients are thoroughly combined.

6. In an electric mixer mixing bowl, combine all of the dry ingredients: tapioca flour through salt. Once these are combined, add the wet ingredients to this bowl and mix on medium speed for 5 minutes.

7. After a nice dough has formed, transfer dough to the prepared loaf pan. Smooth it out with wet fingers and then cover and leave alone to rise for an hour.

8. While it is rising you can take your remaining egg and whisk it together with 1 tsp of water. After the hour of the dough rising, brush the top of the bread with this egg mixture and then sprinkle the rest of the sesame seeds on top.

9. Place in oven and bake for 30 minutes, remove from oven, carefully take bread out of pan, then place back in oven directly on wire rack for another 12 minutes. Remove from oven and place on rack to cool for at least an hour.

10. Enjoy.

Tortillas

Ingredients:

2 cups homemade flour blend
1 tsp baking powder
½ tsp salt
2 tbsp butter, cold, diced
1 cup water, hot

Directions:

1. Combine dry ingredients of flour, baking powder, and salt in mixing bowl. Add in diced butter pieces and work with hands until worked into the size of peas.

2. Slowly add hot water, working it in, and form into a bowl. Keep kneading until it reaches your desired smoothness.

3. Divide dough into 8 even sized pieces and then form each piece into a tight ball with your hands.

4. Roll out each ball until it is shaped into a tortilla.

5. Lightly grease a skillet over medium heat. Place each tortilla onto skillet and let cook for 2 minutes per side, or until each side it slightly golden.

6. Enjoy.

White Bread

Ingredients:

1 tbsp active dry yeast
3 tbsp white sugar
1 ¼ cups warm water
1 1/3 cups rice flour
2/3 cup sorghum flour
½ cup potato starch
½ cup cornstarch
1/3 cup vegetable oil
3 eggs
1 tbsp xanthan gum
1 tsp salt

Directions:

1. Prepare a loaf baking pan by greasing it.

2. Pour the active dry yeast in a bowl with the warm water and sugar. Set aside until it becomes foamy, about 5-7 minutes.

3. Once yeast has activated after 5-7 minutes, combine this along with all of the other ingredients into an electric mixer bowl and turn on medium speed for 3 minutes. Everything should be well incorporated.

4. Spoon into the pre-greased loaf pan and wet your fingers to smooth out the top.

5. Set aside for an hour to allow the dough to rise.

6. Preheat oven to 375 F.

7. Place in oven and let bake for 25 minutes, until it has a nice golden brown color.

8. Remove from oven and let cool in loaf pan until you can remove it comfortably and then let it cool on its own.

Dessert Breads

Cinnamon Raisin Bread

Ingredients:

1 cup water, warm
2 ½ tbsp. brown sugar
1 pack, active dry yeast
4 egg whites
1 cup potato starch
½ cup tapioca flour
¾ cup brown rice flour
½ cup white rice flour
¼ cup flax seed meal
1 ½ tsp xanthan gum
1 tsp guar gum
1 ½ tsp ground cinnamon
¾ tsp salt
2 tsp apple cider vinegar
¼ cup olive oil
½ cup raisins

Directions:

1. Grease a loaf baking pan.

2. Combine the warmed water, brown sugar, and yeast in a cup and set aside for about 5 minutes, until it becomes foamy.

3. In an electric mixer bowl beat egg whites on high for about 30 seconds. Then add olive oil,

apple cider vinegar, and yeast water mixture and mix at low speed for another 30 seconds.

4. In a separate bowl, combine all of the dry ingredients, potato starch through salt, until thoroughly mixed together. Once combined, add these dry ingredients to the bowl containing the wet ingredients all together. Mix on low for a minute or until everything is combined, and then beat on high for a minute. After a minute, mix raisins into the dough using a spatula or dough hook.

5. Place dough into the pre-greased loaf pan. Smooth out with wet fingers until everything is even in the pan. Once smooth, place in a warm area for 45 minutes to rise.

6. Preheat oven to 375 F.

7. Place loaf pan in oven once it reaches 375 F and bake for 40 minutes.

8. Remove from oven, place on cooling rack, and remove loaf from pan as soon as you are able to without burning yourself and let the bread cool on the rack.

9. Enjoy.

Coffee Cake

Ingredients:

For Cake

¼ cup butter, softened
1 egg, beaten
½ cup almond milk
1 tsp vanilla
1 ½ cup homemade gluten free flour blend
¾ cup sugar
2 tsp baking powder
Pinch of salt

For Crumble Topping

½ cup brown sugar
2 tbsp homemade gluten free flour blend
2 tsp ground cinnamon
2 tbsp butter, melted
½ cup walnuts, chopped (optional)

For Frosting Drizzle

½ cup confectioner's sugar
½ tsp vanilla
1 tbsp almond milk

Directions:

1. Preheat oven to 375 F.

2. Grease an 8x8 baking pan.

3. In a mixing bowl, combine the softened butter, beaten egg, almond milk, and vanilla.

4. In a separate bowl combine the remaining cake ingredients until everything is well combined.

5. Slowly add the dry ingredients to the wet ingredients until they are thoroughly incorporated. Pour the batter into the pre-greased baking pan and smooth out.

6. Combine all of the crumble topping ingredients thoroughly in a small mixing bowl. Sprinkle over the top of the batter in the baking pan.

7. Place in the oven and let bake for 25 minutes. After 25 minutes, remove from oven, and let cool. While cake is cooling, combine the frosting ingredients and sprinkle over the top of the cake evenly.

8. Eat up!

Lemon Poppy Seed Bread

Ingredients:

Bread:

2 cups blanched almond flour
2 tsp baking powder
8 tbsp poppy seeds
1 cup sugar
3 eggs
¾ cup + 1 tbsp whole milk
½ cup vegetable oil
½ lemon, only using fresh squeezed juice
1 tsp lemon zest
1 tsp vanilla
1 tsp butter extract
½ tsp salt

Frosting:

1/3 cup butter, melted
2 cup powdered sugar
1 tsp almond extract
3 tbsp water

Directions:

1. In a large mixing bowl combine the almond flour, baking powder, poppy seeds, sugar, and salt.

2. In a separate large mixing bowl beat the eggs and combine with the vegetable oil, lemon juice, zest, vanilla and butter extract.

3. Now you are going to add the dry ingredients to the wet ingredients, a little at a time, and each time adding a little milk. We want to add slowly so lets do it in 4 times. So add ¼ dry ingredients to wet followed by ¼ of the milk and mix together. Then repeat this 3 more times.

4. Preheat oven to 350 F.

5. Grease loaf pan(s) and fill ¾ of the way to top with dough mixture.

6. Place loaf pan in oven and bake for 35 minutes. The goal is to have the whole loaf bake evenly, so that the edges do not brown or burn. Play with oven temperature if this does seem to happen.

7. While baking, mix the frosting ingredients together in a bowl.

8. As bread is finished baking, remove from oven, set on rack while still in pan, and poke tiny holes all over with a fork. Pour the frosting over the entire loaf and let it soak in for some time before removing it from the pan and enjoying!

Pumpkin Bread

Ingredients:

¾ cup brown sugar
¼ cup butter. softened
1 cup canned pumpkin
2 eggs
½ cup low fat buttermilk
¼ cup maple syrup
2 cups homemade flour blend
2 tsp baking powder
½ tsp salt
½ tsp cinnamon
½ tsp ground nutmeg
¼ tsp baking soda
¼ tsp ground cloves

Directions:

1. Preheat oven to 350 F.

2. Grease a loaf pan.

3. In a large mixing bowl, combine the sugar and softened butter and beat together thoroughly. Add the pumpkin, eggs, buttermilk, and maple syrup to the sugar mixture.

4. In a separate bowl, combine all of the remaining ingredients and mix together. Once mixed, add this bowl to the bowl containing wet ingredients and mix until they are thoroughly incorporated.

5. Pour dough into the pre-greased loaf pan.

6. Plan into oven for 60 minutes to let bake. After the hour, remove from oven and let cool until you are able to remove bread from pan, then let cool on its own until you ready to enjoy.

Yellow Cake

Ingredients:

Will yield 2, 8 inch round layers

1 ½ cups white rice flour
¾ cup tapioca flour
1 tsp salt
1 tsp baking soda
3 tsp baking powder
1 tsp xanthan gum
4 eggs
1 ¼ cups white sugar
2/3 cup mayonnaise
1 cup milk
2 tsp vanilla extract

Directions:

1. Preheat oven to 350 F.

2. Grease and spread rice flour on 2, 8 inch round cake pans.

3. Combine the dry ingredients, white rice flour through xanthan gum, in a large mixing bowl.

4. In a separate mixing bowl whisk together the eggs, sugar, and mayonnaise until it has a nice fluff to it. Once it is fluffy, add the dry ingredients from the other mixing bowl, along with the milk and vanilla. Mix together until everything is thoroughly combined.

5. Pour batter mixture evenly into the pre-greased cake pans. Place in oven and let bake for 25 minutes or until cakes have a nice bounce to them when poked.

6. Remove from oven and let cool. Add whatever frostings or toppings you are in the mood for!

Conclusion

There you have it!

My favorite gluten free bread recipes all in one place!

My goal in writing this book was to give hope to the people suffering from celiac and other gluten sensitivities. I know from second hand experience watching my sister struggle that it's not easy to go through something like that. However, with some patience and creativity you can still enjoy the little things in life, such as these delicious bread recipes.

I wish you the best in your health.

Made in the USA
Lexington, KY
13 April 2017